The Antichrist

The Untold Truth:
A Prophetic Synopsis

Daniel Osorio

The Antichrist
Copyright © 2010 by Daniel Osorio

The biblical passages that have been included throughout this book will be in the ALT, CEV, ESV, NIV, or in the NKJV Bible version.

This Book can be ordered through ONLINE booksellers or by contacting: Info@DanielOsorio.org

ISBN: 978-1-4507-5739-3

Also available in ebook format.

LOC#: 2011900779

Printed in the United States of America

Note: The biblical passages that are stated throughout this book are in the Analytical-Living Translation (ALT), Contemporary

English version (CEV), English Standard Version (ESV), New International Version (NIV), or in the New King James Version (NKJV) Bible format.

Table of Contents

Chapter One

INTRODUCTION

As the author of this book, I have felt compelled to write about the purpose of certain events that have been taking place during our present day. These events, ranging from the fluctuations of our worldwide economy to what some have considered normal or natural occurrences, have undoubtedly increased in these days beyond what we have ever witnessed. The increase in natural disasters such as earthquakes, hurricanes, tsunamis, and floods, not to mention the rise in murders, suicides, international terrorism, plagues, and so on, is just the beginning of sorrows. However, the focus of this book is on the people, New York City, and the appearance and deceptions of the Antichrist. I strongly recommend that you neither lose focus, nor set aside the importance of this message, nor accept the so-called normality of these worldwide events, for they will indisputably continue to come about not only because of our government's irresponsibility, but also because of our own choices.

Therefore, I recommend that you read the entire contents of this book, for it was written and given with much love in order to help edify and protect you not only from the things that are now, but also from those that are about to come. Be reassured, however, that what you will read here is the truth, for what I have written pertains to only a few of the many things that I have received with regard to both present and end-time events that will soon take place not only in New York City but throughout the world as well.

Chapter Two

THE ECONOMIC DILEMMA

Our fluctuating economy, which is presently one of our main concerns and is spoken of daily by the media, has moved to a level of troubling instability. Today, the Great Depression of 1929— the Crash—is a painful memory for those who survived it. In essence, we should take into account the events of that day, which serve both as a matter of historical interest and as a warning of future pain and suffering. For it was once established that our government was to never get involved or interfere with the free enterprise economic system. This advice, as well as the warnings of an impending judgment, which many have prophesied throughout the years, has not only been ignored but is also presently being dismissed. The borrowing, overspending, and inflation of our economy by the government may cause us to enter into an economic dilemma. We may blame the leaders of America, but if we, the nations of this world, examine our morals and spiritual values and accept self-blame for this unprecedented predicament, we will comprehend that its cause is not primarily our government's incompetent decisions, but our own ungodly choices. Therefore, unless an appropriate level of godliness becomes evident throughout the churches, America, and the nations of the world, be assured that any efforts to stabilize the economic crisis will unfortunately result in failure.

Accordingly, with regard to the fluctuation and instability of our nation's financial system, could it be that we are once again on the verge of another Great Depression?

Will hyperinflation (the printing of additional currency) reduce the value of our nation's dollar to a worthless penny? Have you compared the value of our dollar with that of the euro? Would the crippling of our economy bring the world's greatest power to the status of a poverty-stricken nation? Will our bank accounts be insured by the federal government? Will government aid be unavailable, due to the severity of an economic calamity? Will law enforcement have control over mass riots?

Certain individuals believe that it is not of great importance to prepare even if there is a warning of impending danger, since they are confident that they will be protected from whatever may come. They quote, but eventually misinterpret, the biblical verse from 1 Thessalonians 5:9, which says, "For God has not appointed us to suffer wrath, but to receive Salvation through our Lord Jesus Christ." Haven't we heard about churchgoing people who suffered during times of catastrophe because they were not prepared? To bring people out of their erroneous belief, I describe below an event that took place in New York City and that had far-reaching effects on many nations.

As many remember, it was an early Tuesday morning on October 29, 1929, since known as "Black Tuesday." As the stock market opened, the traders went about doing business, not suspecting what was to take place on that day. Suddenly, the market crashed, resulting in chaos, bankruptcy, unemployment, poverty, hunger, suicides, and destruction of families throughout the United States and the world, traumatically changing the lives of many. A depression had begun (research the Great Depression of 1929). But I would like to ask several important questions: First, how many people, or even God's messengers, warned about that coming day? Second, how many believed, listened, and were protected because they took action beforehand? Third, how many people searched for food in the streets and in garbage cans in order to survive? Fourth, what would prevent this from happening again? The answer is simple: Nothing! For the people of all nations and religious denominations have become more sinful than ever before, and are provoking God to judgment.

We must all come to understand that we are now living in a time of uncertainty. Our government, despite its deception, lies, corruption, and overspending, should not be held completely accountable for any disaster that will unfortunately be visited upon our nation. As Second Chronicles 7:14 states, "If My people who are called by My name will humble themselves, and pray and seek My face, and turn from their wicked ways, then I will hear from heaven, and will forgive their sin and heal their land."

So I strongly urge that you pay close attention to what is taking place throughout the world and acknowledge the messengers who have been stating, "God warns us to prepare for what is to come." This is the same way that God revealed what was to come to Noah, Joseph, Isaiah, and the many others who have warned of a coming judgment. Read Chapter Three, New York and America: The Great Babylon and Chapter Eleven, The Antichrist: A Prophetic Synopsis.

Chapter Three

NEW YORK AND AMERICA: THE GREAT BABYLON

One day as I focused on the book of Revelation, I came across a couple of chapters that seem to validate several dreams* I'd had that pertained not only to America, but also to the event that occurred in New York City on September 11, 2001. Given the fact that this was a day of terror, distress, and sorrow for many, it is of great importance that we value the memory of those who lost their lives on that day, giving special recognition and admiration to those who served and protected our people, city, and nation. We should also extend unceasing love and sympathy to all who lost a loved one, not neglecting their needs or forgetting the pain and suffering stemming from their loss. But as we continue in this effort, we should never forget that the word of God must be spoken and taught in its truth and never neglected, regardless of past, present, or future circumstances.

In the following passages from Revelation 18, notice how the writer, during his vision, seems to be describing New York City, or even America itself, as "Babylon the Great." For many years, it has been stated that New York is considered a great city, if not one of the greatest cities in the world. Yet it has a reputation as a present-day Sodom and Gomorrah, a city where abomination lies, a sinful place that has not turned from its wicked ways despite the many warnings about its impending Day of Judgment. Detestable sins have piled up to the skies. The people have no fear of God, but continue in idolatry, envy, greed, jealousy, pride in their luxuries, adultery, fornication, freedom of homosexuality, and the parading of such (Leviticus 20:13, Romans 1:26–27, and 1 Corinthians 6:9). Lawmakers have no problem celebrating and allowing Halloween festivities rather than the Nativity, or preventing our children from pledging allegiance to our own U.S. flag or repeating any other pledge that includes the name of God, not acknowledging that removing the Ten Commandments from our U.S. courtrooms will not only harm our nation, but themselves as well.

As you begin to read these paragraphs, notice the key verses from Revelation 18 that seem to describe certain events that took place on September 11, 2001. But as you closely study the verses within the chapter, you will come to realize that the sinful conditions and values described in these passages are closely related to the excess materialism found in New York City or America itself.

A few years before the World Trade Center buildings collapsed, people said that New York City was a safe place to be. They boasted about her luxuries, stating that the Twin Tower buildings were extremely stable and would never be brought down. But as you may recall, at that very hour, the plague of fire brought New York City down (Revelation 18:8), leaving one tower to become a "widow," since one fell before the other. And when Revelation 18:7 states, "I sit as Queen," could it be describing New York City, the Twin Towers, the Statue of Liberty, or just another place? So I ask, pay close attention to the key details of the events within this chapter, for they will broaden your understanding of their relationship with the events of that day.

During the time of their destruction, the collapse of these towers unleashed a blast of harmful dust that up to this day has caused serious consequences, bringing a plague of sickness, and in some cases, death, to those who inhaled it. And although several individuals have believed that the beginning verses of this chapter signify the complete destruction of a city, as you turn to verse 21 you will be able to acknowledge that this assumption is incorrect, since the place of which this verse speaks seems to be facing its ultimate destruction at that very time.

*Consider the book, The Wrath, The Return, The Truth: Judgment Has Begun!

1. As you read, ask yourself if the verses in the following passages from Revelation 18 could be describing the United States or New York City and the destruction of the World Trade Center buildings. Could verse 3 be referring to the stock market of New York City, since the kings and the merchants of the earth have participated not only in America's "power of her luxurious living," but also in New York City's riches? Is there any other place like America that has taken pride in her luxuries?

Revelation 18:3—For all nations have drunk the wine of the passion of her sexual immorality, and the kings of the earth have committed immorality with her, and the merchants of the earth have grown rich from the power of her luxurious living.

Revelation 18:7—As she glorified herself and lived in luxury, so give her a like measure of torment and mourning, since in her heart she says, "I sit as a queen, I am no widow, and mourning I shall never see."

2. Several individuals have assumed that the verses below seem to describe a city that is being destroyed. However, if you relate these verses, along with verse 21, to the destruction of the World Trade Center, you will notice that this is a mistaken assumption because the destruction is not evident until verse 21. Yet, as you continue to read these passages, you will notice that certain verses describe a market of goods. Could these verses be describing the stock market of New York City? Or do they appear to be describing another place? Could Revelation 18:15-19 be describing the occurrences of that day?

Revelation 18:8-13—For this reason her plagues will come in a single day, death and mourning and famine, and she will be burned up with fire; for mighty is the Lord God who has judged her. And the kings of the earth, who committed sexual immorality and lived in luxury with her, will weep and wail over her when they see the smoke of her burning. They will stand far off, in fear of her torment, and say, "Alas! Alas! You great city, you mighty city, Babylon! For in a single hour your judgment has come." And the merchants of the earth weep and mourn for her, since no one buys their cargo anymore, cargo of gold, silver, jewels, pearls, fine linen, purple cloth, silk, scarlet cloth, all kinds of scented wood, all kinds of articles of ivory, all kinds of articles of costly wood, bronze, iron and marble, cinnamon, spice, incense, myrrh, frankincense, wine, oil, fine flour, wheat, cattle and sheep, horses and chariots, and slaves, that is, human souls.

Revelation 18:15-19—The merchants of these wares, who gained wealth from her, will stand far off, in fear of her torment, weeping and mourning aloud, "Alas, alas, for the great city that was clothed in fine linen, in purple and scarlet, adorned with gold, with jewels, and with pearls! For in a single hour all this wealth has been laid waste." And all shipmasters and seafaring men, sailors and all whose trade is on the sea, stood far off and cried out as they saw the smoke of her burning, "What city was like the great city?" And they threw dust on their heads as they wept and mourned, crying out, "Alas, alas, for the great city where all who had ships at sea grew rich by her wealth! For in a single hour she has been laid waste."

3. Now, according to the above verses and the events that were revealed* to me, could this be one of the unfortunate events that is to come upon New York City? Notice that when the mighty angel takes a "stone like a great millstone" and throws it into the sea, the city "will be found no more." Doesn't this appear to be describing destruction from a tsunami or a massive flood?

Revelation 18:21-23—Then a mighty angel took up a stone like a great millstone and threw it into the sea, saying, "So will Babylon the great city be thrown down with violence, and will be found no more; and the sound of harpists and musicians, of flute players and trumpeters, will be heard in you no more, and a craftsman of any craft will be found in you no more, and the sound of the mill will be heard in you no more, and the light of a lamp will shine in you no more, and the voice of bridegroom and bride will be heard in you no more, for your merchants were the great ones of the earth, and all nations were deceived by your sorcery."

From this account, could we conclude that the passages from the second illustration are referring to the time of the city's destruction?

To further support this conclusion, the following passages will focus on a possible interpretation of what the Bible states with regard to New York City and America. But let it be known that even prior to my having stumbled upon these passages and obtaining their accompanying interpretation, the descriptions contained in them were relevant to a few of my past and present dreams.

Now, in reading the following verses, found in Revelation 17, along with the interpretations provided below each verse, you will gain insight into how "Babylon the Great" seems to closely resemble New York and even America. To provide additional insight into the following passages, Hal Lindsey, a well-known television preacher who teaches about eschatology (end time), wrote, "We are at the moment, the most powerful nation on earth, by every conceivable measure. But in all fairness, we should reflect carefully, and with an open mind, in order to determine whether the following passages and accompanying interpretations are actually referring to this nation or to another.

Revelation 17:1—Then one of the seven angels who had the seven bowls came and talked with me, saying to me, "Come, I will show you the judgment of the great harlot who sits on many waters."

As you compare this passage with Revelation 17:15, you will become aware that "the great harlot who sits on many waters" represents peoples, multitudes, nations, and tongues.

Revelation 17:4-5—The woman was arrayed in purple and scarlet, and adorned with gold and precious stones and pearls, having in her hand a golden cup full of abominations and the filthiness of her fornication. And on her forehead a name was written: mystery, Babylon the Great, the mother of harlots and of the abominations of the earth.

Revelation 17:15—Then he said to me, "The waters which you saw, where the harlot sits, are peoples, multitudes, nations, and tongues."

Could the "peoples, multitudes, nations, and tongues" spoken about in the above verse be referring to a nation other than the United States? Do we not know of the many people from other nationalities who have preferred to migrate to the United States rather than to any other country because of its freedom and opportunities? Are we not aware of the legal battles this country has been facing because of the vast number of immigrants taking up residence throughout our nation?

Revelation 17:16—And the ten horns which you saw on the beast, these will hate the harlot, make her desolate and naked, eat her flesh and burn her with fire.

With regard to the above, could this be one of the unfortunate events that is to come upon New York and/or America? Have we known of any other nation on the earth that has been as disliked or hated as the United States?

To obtain the meaning of the "Ten Horns," read Daniel 7:24 and Revelation 17:12.

Revelation 17:18—And the woman whom you saw is that great city which reigns over the kings of the earth."

Although the United States has not necessarily been regarded as reigning over the kings or the nations of the earth, we cannot overlook the fact that for many years America, more than any other nation, has been considered the superpower of the world. Do we know of any other nation with as much power, and as abundant in riches and weaponry, as America?

New York City and America, yes, you are what the Bible describes as "Babylon the Great." A "great city" that will not be uprooted as it was, a beautiful city that has held many up because of its riches. All nations will mourn because of you, a mourning of darkness that, because of the abominations which are also being committed throughout the world, will cause many to be brought to their knees and to suffer. Read Isaiah 3:18-26 and Amos 8:9-10.

Jeremiah 25:29-32—For behold, I begin to work disaster at the city that is called by My name, and shall you go unpunished? You shall not go unpunished, for I am summoning a sword AGAINST ALL THE INHABITANTS OF THE EARTH, declares the Lord of hosts.' "You, therefore, shall prophesy against them all these words, and say to them: "'The Lord will roar from on high, and from His holy habitation utter His voice; He will roar mightily against His fold, and shout, like those who tread grapes, AGAINST ALL THE INHABITANTS OF THE EARTH. The clamor will resound to the ends of the earth, for the Lord has an indictment against the nations; He is ENTERING INTO JUDGMENT WITH ALL FLESH, and the wicked He will put to the sword, declares the Lord.' "Thus says the Lord of hosts: Behold, disaster is going forth from nation to nation, and a great tempest is stirring from the farthest parts of the earth!

Be forewarned, as soon as New York's economic market comes to its ultimate demise, the United States, together with the rest of the world, will without a doubt come into a Great Depression worse than the one that took place in 1929. This economic collapse, according to biblical description and prophecy, will bring about another major event unequal to any other (read Chapter 11, The Antichrist: A Prophetic Synopsis). But how unfortunate that many have disregarded the warnings, failing to acknowledge that the deficits, overspending, and corruption taking place throughout many local, city, state, and federal agencies, as well as the lack of employment and higher prices, will also be among the causes that will eventually lead to the economic downfall and other events. Be assured, problems are coming, and they're going to get worse!

Chapter Four

THE RETURN:
A BIBLICAL PERSPECTIVE

For centuries, many individuals have believed that a supernatural event, presumed to occur sometime in the near future, will surpass any other since the creation of the world. This event has been criticized by many because it is to lead up to the disappearance of hundreds of thousands of people. Although its timing is not known, Christians and members of other religions throughout the world continue to hold on to this belief and the truth of people being taken from this earth sometime in the near future.

Many have dedicated themselves theologically to studying, and eventually writing, books that pertain to the Great Tribulation and the arrival of the Antichrist. While their focus is primarily on the second coming of the Lord, the first resurrection or gathering (rapture) of His people, they also speculate as to what point in the Bible these events will take place. The majority of the people within the church have preached, taught, and accepted that God's chosen people will be taken before the Great Tribulation (pre-tribulation); others believe that it will happen within the first three and a half years of the seven-year tribulation (mid-tribulation). Still others believe that it will take place after the seven years have been completed (post-tribulation). And, claiming that the Bible states otherwise, many do not accept the mid- or post-tribulation rapture, believing instead that the church will be exempt from such an event. In an attempt to clear up this confusion and settle the controversy, I have written a brief but detailed description—not from a theological point of view but from a biblical and spiritual perspective— of an approximate point within the Great Tribulation when it seems these events will take place.

You will notice that, in certain books of the Old Testament, the Tribulation was revealed to a few of the prophets, and it was spoken and taught with clarity by Jesus Christ Himself in the New Testament. Its occurrence was widely and boldly circulated by certain apostles, disciples, and

Christians after His death and resurrection. Through their teachings they announce that this event, which many have called "the rapture," will only include those who have accepted and held on to the true faith and doctrine of Jesus Christ. However, certain individuals have misinterpreted the fourth chapter of Revelation as being the rapture of the church simply because of what was told to John in verse 1, "Come up here." They believe that these words symbolize the resurrection or rapture of God's people. It is suggested, however, that you not quote or accept one biblical verse as proof to one's belief, in order to avoid confusion or contradiction when referring to other passages on the same topic.

Nevertheless, what should be understood is that the word "rapture" is not found in any of the original translations of the Bible (KJV, NKJV, etc.), nor is it an actual biblical word. The term that is commonly used to refer to this event is the "first resurrection." This word, although misinterpreted, occurs throughout several New Testament scriptures, and also refers to Christ's coming (His second coming) and the gathering together of God's people. Yet another phrase commonly used to refer to this event is "in the twinkling of an eye." It is located in 1 Corinthians 15:52, which states, "In a moment, in the twinkling of an eye, at the last trumpet. For the trumpet will sound, and the dead will be raised incorruptible, and we shall be changed." Found in several Old and New Testament books, "the Day of the Lord" is still another phrase that refers to this event and that can also be misinterpreted. But one final word that I have found to be of interest and utmost importance in describing this event is the word "Harvest." This word was mainly spoken and defined by Christ Himself and was used as a symbol of the actual "rapture," unlike the aforementioned terms. These references can be found in Matthew 9:37 and 38, Matthew 13:30 and 39, as well as Revelation 14:15-16.

Chapter Five

THE CHRONOLOGICAL EVENTS

In 1 Corinthians 15:23, you will read about certain key events that occur before the coming of Christ and the rapture of His people. But as I began to read different versions of the Bible, I noticed that this verse also reads, "Christ the firstfruits; afterward those who are Christ's at His Coming." As I compared this verse with certain other biblical passages*, I became aware that the proper order seems to be, "Christ, the firstfruits, afterward those who are Christ's at His coming." So to help provide understanding of this verse, below you will read a brief analysis, along with the biblical passage that corresponds to each event. But I ask that you pay close attention to the capitalized word (Coming) within these passages, for it will give evidence supporting the belief in the events of the Great Tribulation, before the time of His (Christ's) Coming. *Read Matthew 27:35, Revelation 14:1-5, Matthew 24:30-31, and Revelation 14:14-16.

1 Corinthians 15:23—But each one in his own order: Christ, the firstfruits, afterward those who are Christ's at HIS COMING.

Several believe that the latter part of 1 Corinthians 15:23 (those who are Christ's at His Coming) refers to those left behind after the taking (rapture) of His people. However, in the Bible, you will find no indication of people being resurrected (raptured) from the earth before the time of Christ's coming. Relate 1 Corinthians 15:23 (the firstfruits and His Coming) with Revelation 14:1-5 and 14:14-16.

Additionally, 1 Corinthians 15:24 disproves this assumption, since it is evident that Christ, after His coming, will hand over all power and authority over to God.

1 Corinthians 15:24—Then comes the end, when He delivers the kingdom to God the Father, when He puts an end to all rule and all authority and power. Compare with Revelation 14:14-20.

A brief summary of 1 Corinthians 15:23

Firstly, the crucifixion and resurrection of Christ.

Secondly, the "firstfruits" refers to the 144,000 of the tribes of Israel (Revelation 14:1-4)."

Thirdly, "those who are Christ's at His Coming" are the chosen who will be taken (raptured) at the time of Christ's coming, as supported in the passages cited throughout these paragraphs.

To support belief in the third event, as you read the following passages, you will notice that the rapture of His people will not occur until the time of Christ's coming, an event which is to occur at the first resurrection, as described in Revelation 20:6. Read the order of events provided in Chapter Seven, The Revelation.

1 Thessalonians 4:15-17—For this we say to you by the word of the Lord, that we who are alive and remain UNTIL THE COMING of the Lord will by no means precede those who are asleep. For the Lord Himself will DESCEND from heaven with a shout, with the voice of an archangel, and with the trumpet of God. And the dead in Christ will rise first. Then we who are alive and remain shall be caught up together with them in the clouds to meet the Lord in the air. And thus we shall always be with the Lord.

1 Thessalonians 5:23—Now may the God of peace Himself sanctify you completely; and may your whole spirit, soul, and body be preserved blameless at the COMING of our Lord Jesus Christ.

Chapter Six

THE CONTROVERSIAL BELIEF

According to the belief of several individuals, the phrase within Revelation 3:10 that states, "I also will keep you from the hour of trial" is considered to denote the resurrection (rapture) of His people, simply because of the word "keep." They have not acknowledged that the next verse states, "Behold, I am COMING quickly! Hold fast what you have, that no one may take your crown." The crown of which this verse speaks will be given only to those who have been found worthy and taken (raptured) at the time of His return, which seems to occur, evidently, after the previous verse (Revelation 3:10) has been fulfilled.

Revelation 3:10—"Because you have kept My command to persevere, I also will keep you from the hour of trial which shall come upon the whole world, to test those who dwell on the earth. Read Chapter Three, "New York and

America: The Great Babylon" and Chapter Eleven, "The Antichrist: A Prophetic Synopsis."

Revelation 3:11—"Behold, I am COMING quickly! Hold fast what you have, that no one may take your crown.

Therefore, if Revelation 3:10 is considered to be the rapture of the church, then it would determine that those who were left behind will be worthy to receive a crown of life. Is this not controversial? Will Christ set a crown on those left behind after He comes to gather (rapture) His people from the earth? And as I said previously, I strongly suggest that you not quote and accept any one verse as the answer to a biblical study, since it may cause confusion or misinterpretation while referencing others within the same subject. Compare Revelation 3:11 (His Coming) with 1 Corinthians 15:23; 1 Thessalonians 4:15-17; 1 Thessalonians 5:23; Matthew 24:30; and Revelation 14:14.

Now, as you read 2 Thessalonians 2:1-4 and 7-12, you will notice that "the Coming of our Lord Jesus Christ and our* gathering (rapture) together to Him" will not occur until "the falling away comes first, and the man of lawlessness (Antichrist) is revealed."

2 Thessalonians 2:1-4—Now, brethren, concerning the COMING of our Lord Jesus Christ and OUR* GATHERING (rapture) together to Him, we ask you, not to be soon shaken in mind or troubled, either by spirit or by word or by letter, as if from us, as though the Day of Christ had come. LET NO ONE DECEIVE YOU by any means; for that Day (His coming and the rapture) WILL NOT COME unless the falling away comes first, and the man of sin IS REVEALED, the son of perdition, who opposes and exalts himself above all that is called God or that is worshiped, so that he sits as God in the temple of God, showing himself that he is God.

Therefore, if Paul was not referring to the actual Coming of Christ and the rapture of His people (2 Thessalonians 2:1), then for what purpose did he include himself* in this event if indeed the rapture had already occurred? Paul's message is that we should not be misled by Satan's lies (2 Thessalonians 2:2-3).

But do not be misled into believing that the verse from 2 Thessalonians 2:7, which states, "only He who now restrains will do so until He is taken out of the way" is referring to the church or the taking (rapture) of God's people. For as we know, the church is not referred to biblically as "He" but as "she," since the "Bridegroom," who is considered to be Christ Himself, will return to receive the church as His bride. Further, if you notice, this verse is not describing the church or its removal, but He who is presently restraining the lawless one, "whom the Lord will consume with the breath of His mouth and destroy with the brightness of HIS COMING."

2 Thessalonians 2:7-12—For the mystery of lawlessness is already at work; only He who now restrains will do so until He is taken out of the way. And then the lawless one will be revealed, whom the Lord will consume with the breath of His mouth and destroy with the brightness of HIS COMING. The coming of the lawless one is according to the working of Satan, with all power, signs, and lying wonders, and with all unrighteous deception among those who perish, because they did not receive the love of the truth, that they might be saved. And for this reason God will send them strong delusion, that they should believe the lie, that they all may be condemned who did not believe the truth but had pleasure in unrighteousness.

And, when you compare these passages (2 Thessalonians 2:7-8) with Matthew 24:30-31, you will notice that the angels will be of those who "will gather together His elect from the four winds, from one end of heaven to the other."

As you compare 2 Thessalonians 2:8 (His coming) with Matthew 24:29-31, Revelation 14:14-16, and Revelation 16:1-15, you will notice a similarity in how this event is described.

Chapter Seven

THE REVELATION

With regard to the "firstfruits" and to "those who are Christ's at His Coming" (1 Corinthians 15:23), as you read Revelation 14, you will notice that the 144,000 of the tribes of Israel (firstfruits) "were [note the use of the past tense] redeemed from the earth" before the mark of the beast (Revelation 14:9-12) and God's people had been "reaped" (raptured) from the earth (Revelation 14:14-16).

Further, as you read Revelation 14:9-12, you will see that a third angel is advising and warning the saints of the consequences of accepting the mark of the beast. And this verse is not intended as a warning toward the Tribes of the 144,000, for if you turn to Revelation 7:3 and 4, you will notice that an angel advises four other angels not to harm the earth until "we have sealed the servants of our God on their foreheads." This seal, which was placed on the 144,000, is not necessarily a seal to protect them from death, but for the purpose of their protection in order to set them apart for God, since they are the "firstfruits" of Christ "who were redeemed from the earth" as described in Revelation 14:3-5, clearly giving us the indication that these 144,000 will not be receiving the "mark or the name of the beast, or the number of his name" (Revelation 13:17).

As you come to Revelation 14:14, you will read of one who looks like a "Son of man," sitting on a white cloud and wearing a crown of gold, Who, as most of us may know, is Christ Himself. For as you read verse 16, you will notice that He (the Lord) reaps the earth's harvest as stated in Matthew 9:37 and 38, Matthew 13:30, and Luke 10:2.

First Event: The 144,000 of the tribes of Israel (firstfruits) "who were redeemed from the earth."

Revelation 14:3-5—They sang as it were a new song before the throne, before the four living creatures, and the elders; and no one could learn that song except the hundred and forty-four thousand who WERE REDEEMED FROM THE EARTH. These are the ones who were not defiled with women, for they are virgins. These are the ones who follow the Lamb wherever He goes. These WERE REDEEMED from among men, being FIRSTFRUITS to God and to the Lamb. And in their mouth was found no deceit, for they are without fault before the throne of God.

Second Event: The mark of the beast that will be placed on those who had accepted him.

Revelation 14:9–12—Then a THIRD angel followed them, saying with a loud voice, "If anyone worships the beast and his image, and receives his mark on his forehead or on his hand, he himself shall also drink of the wine of the wrath of God, which is poured out full strength into the cup of His indignation. He shall be tormented with fire and brimstone in the presence of the holy angels and in the presence of the Lamb. And the smoke of their torment ascends forever and ever; and they have no rest day or night, who worship the beast and his image, and whoever receives the mark of his name." Here is the patience of the saints; here are those who keep the commandments of God and the FAITH OF JESUS.

With regard to the above, could there be any other "saints" to which this verse (Revelation 14:12) could be referring if one has already been "sealed" (Revelation 7:4) and "redeemed" (Revelation 14:3) by the angels of God? Aren't the multitude of Revelation 7:9 considered saints as well? Isn't this a warning for these other chosen people of God (the church)?

Third Event: The Coming of Christ appearing on a cloud to reap (rapture) of the earth's harvest, which will evidently occur after the 144,000 are "redeemed from the earth" (Revelation 14:3-5) and the mark of the beast is being placed on the people (Revelation 14:9-12). *Compare with Acts 1:9-11 and Matthew 24:29-31.

Revelation 14:14–16—Then I looked, and behold, a white cloud, and on the cloud* sat One like the Son of Man (Jesus Christ), having on His head a golden crown, and in His hand a sharp sickle. And another angel came out of the temple, crying with a loud voice to Him who sat on the cloud, "Thrust in Your sickle and reap, for the time has come for You to reap, for the harvest of the earth is ripe." So He who sat on the cloud thrust in His sickle on the earth, and the earth was reaped. See also Matthew 13:30 and 39.

Fourth Event: The full wrath of God that will come upon those who were not taken (raptured) at the time of Christ's coming.

Revelation 14:17-20—Then another angel came out of the temple which is in heaven, he also having a sharp sickle. And another angel came out from the altar, who had power over fire, and he cried with a loud cry to him who had the sharp sickle, saying, "Thrust in your sharp sickle and gather the clusters of the vine of the earth, for her grapes are fully ripe." So the angel thrust his sickle into the earth and gathered the vine of the earth, and threw it into the great winepress of the wrath of God. And the winepress was trampled outside the city, and blood came out of the winepress, up to the horses' bridles, for one thousand six hundred furlongs.

In evaluating the above passages and those from Revelation 20, 4-6 and 11-15, you will become aware that only one redemption and two resurrections will occur. This redemption will only include those from the 144,000 of the Tribes of

Israel as described in Revelation 14:1-3. And those who will take part in the first resurrection will be those as described in Daniel 12:1-11, Matthew 24:30-31, 2 Thessalonians 2:1-5, Revelation 14:14-16, and Revelation 16:15. But those who were not taken in the first will unfortunately take part in the second resurrection because of their unworthiness or because they have eventually taken the mark of the beast. These will be those who face the danger of the second death (lake of fire) as described in Revelation 20:15.

Therefore, if the Coming of the Lord is to occur at the first resurrection and not at the redemption or the second resurrection, then it is clear that the rapture will not occur until a time of Tribulation has taken place, as described in Matthew 24:29-31, 2 Thessalonians 2:1-5, and Revelation 14:1-16. As you search the Bible, you will find no indication that the first resurrection (His Coming and the rapture) will occur before a time of Tribulation. So, unless the redemption of the 144000 and the Great Tribulation are found to occur after His Coming and the gathering (rapture) of His people, I suggest you reconsider these beliefs. Relate Acts 1:9-11 with Matthew 24:29-31 and Revelation 14:1-16.

As you read the following passages from Daniel 11 and 12, notice the capitalized words and the information Daniel receives about times of tribulation that will occur before the resurrection (rapture) of God's people comes about. For as we know, it is biblically evident that "those who remain "faithful" to God will be among the worthy who will be eventually taken (raptured) from the earth.

Daniel 11:31-36—He will send troops to pollute the temple and the fortress, and he will stop the daily sacrifices. Then he will set up that "Horrible Thing" that causes destruction. The king will USE DECEIT to win followers from those who are UNFAITHFUL to God, but THOSE WHO REMAIN FAITHFUL will do everything possible to oppose him. Wise leaders will instruct many of the people. But for a while, some of these leaders will either be killed with swords or burned alive, or else robbed of their possessions and thrown into prison. They will receive only a little help in their time of trouble, and many of their followers will be treacherous. Some of those who are wise will suffer, so that GOD WILL MAKE THEM PURE AND ACCEPTABLE until the end, which will still come at the time He has decided. This king will do as he pleases. He will proudly claim to be greater than any god and will insult the only true God(2 Thessalonians 2:3-4). Indeed, he will be successful until GOD IS NO LONGER ANGRY WITH HIS PEOPLE.

Daniel 12:1-4—"At that time Michael shall stand up, The great prince who stands watch over the sons of your people; And there shall be A TIME OF TROUBLE, such as never was since there was a nation, Even to that time. And at that time your people shall be delivered, every one who is found written in the book. And MANY OF THOSE who sleep in the dust of the earth shall awake, some to everlasting life, some to shame and everlasting contempt. THOSE WHO ARE WISE SHALL SHINE LIKE THE BRIGHTNESS OF THE FIRMAMENT, AND THOSE WHO TURN MANY TO RIGHTEOUSNESS LIKE THE STARS FOREVER AND EVER. "But you, Daniel, shut up the words, and seal the book until the time of the end; many shall run to and fro, and knowledge shall increase."

Daniel 12:6-7—And one said to the man clothed in linen, who was above the waters of the river, "How long shall the fulfillment of these wonders be?" Then I heard the man clothed in linen, who was above the waters of the river, when he held up his right hand and his left hand to heaven, and swore by Him who lives forever, that it shall be for a time, times, and half a time (3 and a half years); and when the power of the HOLY PEOPLE has been completely shattered, all these things shall be finished.

Therefore, will "holy people" (Daniel 12:7) be left behind to face the Great Tribulation while other people ARE raptured from the earth? Is this not controversial?

To further support the evidence of this belief as well as that of the three and a half years (time, times, and half a time), as you read Revelation 13:7, you will be able to see how the Antichrist was "granted to make war with the saints and to overcome them" for 42 months (three and a half years), as spoken about in verse 5. But notice the latter part of verse 7, which states, "And authority was given him over every tribe, tongue, and nation." As you compare this passage with passages in Revelation 14, it will become clear that the "saints" mentioned in verse 7 are not from the 144,000 of the tribes of the children of Israel. Nor is this a reference to the Israelite nation itself, but to "every (all) tribe, tongue (language), and nation of the world."

Revelation 13:5-7—And he was given a mouth speaking great things and blasphemies, and he was given authority to continue for forty-two months (3 and a half years). Then he opened his mouth in blasphemy against God, to blaspheme His name, His tabernacle, and those who dwell in heaven. It was granted to him to make war with the saints and to overcome them. And authority was given him over every tribe, tongue, and nation.

Revelation 13:8-10—All who dwell on the earth will worship him, whose names have not been written in the Book of Life of the Lamb slain from the foundation of the world. If anyone has an ear, let him hear. He who leads into captivity shall go into captivity; he who kills with the sword must be killed with the sword. Here is the patience and the faith of the saints.

With regard to these passages, could we conclude, then, that the gathering (rapture) of His people will not occur until a time of Tribulation has taken place? Will "holy people" (Daniel 12:7) or "saints" (Revelation 13:10) be left behind after Christ comes to gather (rapture) His people from the earth?

In the following verses from Daniel 12, notice the word "blessed" and how it seems to be giving us evidence of the Great Tribulation, to confirm the hope of one "who waits" forty-five days after the daily sacrifice has been abolished and the abomination of desolation is set up (take 1,290 days from 1,335 days). Could the phrase "**Blessed is he** who waits" be referring to this forty-five-day period associated with the coming of the Lord and the gathering (rapture) of His people?

As you study these passages along with those in Revelation 14, 20, and 19, it will become evident that they are describing the expectancy of that event. Daniel 12:11 states, "And from the time that the daily sacrifice is taken away, and the abomination of desolation is set up, there shall be one thousand two hundred and ninety days." Daniel 12:12 says, "**Blessed is he** who waits, and comes to the one thousand three hundred and thirty-five days." And Revelation 14:13 states, "**Blessed** are the dead who die in the Lord from now on." "Yes, says the Spirit, that they may rest from their labors, and their works follow them." Then Revelation 20:6 states, "**Blessed and Holy** (Daniel 12:7) **is he** who has part in the first resurrection. Over such the second death has no power, but they shall be priests of God and of Christ, and shall reign with Him a thousand years." And again, in Revelation 19:9: "Then He said to me, 'Write: "**Blessed** are those who are called to the marriage supper of the Lamb!"'" And He said to me, 'These are the true sayings of God."See also Revelation 1:3, 16:15, and 22:7.

Revelation 22:14—Blessed are those who do His commandments, that they may have the right to the tree of life, and may enter through the gates into the city.

Are you now able to acknowledge that the "blessed...who waits" for the forty-five-day period during the time of the Great Tribulation will be of those who will be resurrected (raptured) from the earth?

Chapter Eight

THE MISCONCEPTION

Many have expected the unusual and extraordinary events of Matthew 24 to take place in the near future, but these occurrences have been widely misinterpreted. I ask that you be attentive to the description and biblical passages provided below. They will broaden your understanding regarding the occurrences of that day.

Comparing Matthew 24:29-31 with Acts 2:19-20, you will notice times of Tribulation that will occur before Christ appears on a cloud to gather His people from the four corners of the earth. Further, when you read Acts 1:9-11 and relate it to other biblical passages, you will find no evidence supporting the belief that Christ will return on a cloud before a time of Tribulation. Again, I ask that you pay close attention to the capitalized words within these passages, for it will give evidence supporting the belief in the events of the Great Tribulation, before the time of His (Christ's) Coming.

Matthew 24:29-31—"Immediately AFTER THE TRIBULATION of those days the sun will be darkened, and the moon will not give its light; the stars will fall from heaven (see also Acts 2:19-20 and Revelation 6:12-17), and the powers of the heavens will be shaken. Then the sign of the Son of Man will appear in heaven, and then all the tribes of the earth will mourn, and they will see the Son of Man COMING ON THE CLOUDS of heaven with power and great glory (see also Acts 1:9-11 and Revelation 14:14-16). And He will send His angels with a great SOUND OF A TRUMPET, and they will gather (rapture) together His elect from the four winds, from one end of heaven to the other."

Acts 2:19-20—"I will show wonders in heaven above and signs in the earth beneath: Blood and fire and vapor of smoke. The sun shall be turned into darkness, and the moon into blood (see also Matthew 24:29-31 and Revelation 6:12-17), BEFORE THE COMING of the great and awesome Day of the Lord.

Matthew 24:40-44—Then two men will be in the field: one will be taken (raptured) and the other left. Two women will be grinding at the mill: one will be taken (raptured) and the other left. Watch therefore, for you do not know what hour your Lord is COMING. Therefore you also be ready, for the Son of Man is COMING at an hour you do not expect.

Acts 1:9-11—Now when He had spoken these things, while they watched, He was taken up, and A CLOUD received Him out of their sight. And while they looked steadfastly toward heaven as He went up, behold, two men stood by them in white apparel, who also said, "Men of Galilee, why do you stand gazing up into heaven? This same Jesus, who was taken up from you into heaven, WILL SO COME IN LIKE MANNER as you saw Him go into heaven."

Have you noticed times of tribulation like those we are warned about before the "awesome Day of the Lord"? Could we conclude, then, that the "awesome Day of the Lord" spoken about in this verse (Acts 2:19-20) seems to be referring to the coming of the Lord and the gathering (rapture) of His people?

Further, if the events of the Sun, Moon, and Stars that are stated in the above passages are relevant to the sixth seal of Revelation 6:12-13, then be assured that the first six seals* of Judgment (Revelation 6) will befall the people of the earth before the coming of the Lord and the gathering (rapture) of His people. *Read Chapter Nine, "The Judgment: A Biblical Synopsis."

Revelation 6:12-13—I looked when He opened the sixth seal, and behold, there was a great earthquake; and the SUN became black as sackcloth of hair, and the MOON became like blood. And the STARS of heaven fell to the earth, as a fig tree drops its late figs when it is shaken by a mighty wind.

Therefore, if Matthew 24:30-31 is not considered the rapture of the church, as many believe, then shouldn't the Bible demonstrate another Coming of Christ—a Christ who would appear on a cloud prior to the one written about in Matthew 24:30-31 and Revelation 14:14-16? Could the fear of having to face tribulation cause one to reject the truth of God's word? Isn't God able to protect His people, just as He protected Noah, Lot, Joseph, and many other righteous servants during times of catastrophe? Again, read Revelation 3:10 and 3:11.

Hosea 4:6—My people are destroyed for lack of knowledge. Because you have rejected knowledge, I also will REJECT YOU FROM BEING PRIEST* for Me; Because you have forgotten the law of your God, I also will forget your children. *Relate with Revelation 20:6 and 2 Timothy 3:15.

It is beyond comprehension how churches can relate certain passages from Matthew 24 to present-day occurrences, but reject others from this chapter because of the belief that the mention of the "gathering of His elect" is not the rapture of the church. If this is the belief, then shouldn't the Coming of Christ and the rapture of His church be evident elsewhere? Since this belief cannot be supported, then who could Christ be gathering from one end of heaven to the other? Could this event be referring to the 144,000 of the tribes of Israel? Weren't these 144,000 "redeemed" (PAST TENSE) from the earth before Christ appeared (Revelation 14:3-4 and 14-16)? Is it not stated in Acts 1:9-11 that Christ will return on a cloud? Isn't it evident that Christ is returning on a cloud in Matthew 24:30 and Revelation 14:14?

So, if the 144,000 of the tribes of Israel "were" already " redeemed from the earth" (Revelation 14:3-4) prior to the mark of the beast, the Coming of the Lord (appearing on a cloud), and the gathering (rapture) of His people (Revelation 14:9-16), then shouldn't this imply that the elect spoken about in Matthew 24:30-31 are not of the 144,000 of the tribes of Israel? Could there be any other people to whom this verse could refer if the 144,000 "were" already "redeemed from the earth"?

Further, if Christ, at His Coming, is to appear on a cloud to rapture His people from the earth, and Matthew 24:29-31 and Revelation 14:14-16 are the only passages referring to this event, what support is there elsewhere in the Bible that the rapture will occur before a time of Tribulation? Isn't the first resurrection the only event referring to Christ's Coming and the rapture of His people?

Therefore, if the rapture of God's people is to occur at the time of Christ's Coming, or the first resurrection, as evident throughout these passages, then be assured that times of Tribulation will unfortunately occur before His people are taken (raptured) from the earth. Compare Acts 1:9-11 with Matthew 24:29-31 and Revelation 14:14-16.

In searching the Bible, you will find no evidence supporting the belief that His people will be taken (raptured) from the earth before the time of His (Christ's) Coming. Again, read the order of events from Revelation 14:3-4 (the redemption of the 144,000) and Revelation 14:9-12 (the arrival of the Antichrist) that will occur before the coming of the Lord and the rapture of His people, as stated in Revelation 14:14-16. Unless proper evidence can be provided supporting the belief of a pre-tribulation rapture, rather than what many have considered and quoted from 1 Thessalonians 5:9 and Revelation 4:1, I suggest you reassess your beliefs, for beliefs alone, without sufficient facts, are not the means to proven evidence.

2 Timothy 4:3-4—For the time is coming when people will not endure sound teaching, but having itching ears they will accumulate for themselves teachers to suit their own passions, and will TURN AWAY FROM LISTENING TO THE TRUTH and wander off into myths.

2 Timothy 3:15—and that from childhood you have known the Holy Scriptures, which are able to make you wise for salvation through faith which is in Christ Jesus. Relate with Hosea 4:6.

We must acknowledge that not only is the word "rapture" not biblical, but also that its occurrence is being taught in a manner that is contrary to the Bible. In essence, it has come to my attention that both the inability to cite this word in the Bible, and the manner in which is being presented, will cause much confusion among the people because of the belief that this rapture, as many call it, will not only occur before the time of Tribulation, but even before Christ's Coming. This is not at all biblical! As Hebrews 9:28 says, "So Christ was offered once to bear the sins of many. To those who eagerly wait for Him He will appear a second time, apart from sin, for salvation." This verse seems to tell us that the gathering (rapture) of His people will not occur until Christ appears for the second time, an event which is foretold in Matthew 24:29-31, 2 Thessalonians 2:1-8, Revelation 14: 1-16, and Revelation 16:1-15. And although believing in a pre-tribulation, mid-tribulation, or post-tribulation coming of the Lord (rapture) will not necessarily cause the loss of one's salvation, be advised that teaching it inappropriately may cause one to believe and accept the deception of the deceiver (Antichrist), which will eventually bring God's judgment upon you. Read Revelation 14:9-11.

Therefore, by this determination, it is evident that the church, despite its rejections and beliefs, will not be taken (raptured) until the time when the mark or the name of the beast, or the number of his name (Revelation 13:17) is being placed on the people as described in Revelation 14:9-16. Reread and compare the order of events from 1 Corinthians 15:23-24, Revelation 14:3-20, and Revelation 16:1-15.

Chapter Nine

THE JUDGMENT:
A BIBLICAL SYNOPSIS

Below I list several Old Testament scriptures of the Bible. They contain the events that were revealed to the prophets of old. These revelations relate to several New Testament scriptures, which correspond to the Day of Judgment and to Christ's return.

As you read these passages, notice how the events being described seem to correspond to events that are to take place before the Coming of the Lord. Also, as you read Joel 2:31, you will notice that this event was revealed to the prophet Isaiah (13:10), and can also be found in Acts 2:19-20, Mark 13:24, and Revelation 6:12. However, notice Amos 5:18-23, Isaiah 13:6-7, and Isaiah 13:9-13, for they describe an event that is called the "Day of the Lord." This day could well represent the day of wrath, but when you read Acts 2:19-20 and relate it to the other passages cited throughout this chapter, I am certain you will be able to determine that this phrase "Day of the Lord" is referring not just to the Day of judgment, as many believe, but also to His Coming. So if the prophecies of Joel 2, Isaiah 13, and Amos 5 and 8 relate with the sixth seal of Revelation 6:12, then it is evident that the first six seals of judgment (Revelation 6) will eventually take place before the Coming of the Lord and the resurrection (rapture) of His people. But pay close attention to the capitalized words within these passages, for they provide evidence supporting the belief of the Great Tribulation, before the time of His (Christ's) Coming.

Joel 2:29-32—And also on My menservants and on My maidservants I will pour out My Spirit in those days. And I will show wonders in the heavens and in the earth: Blood and fire and pillars of smoke. The sun shall be turned into darkness, and the moon into blood, BEFORE THE COMING of the great and awesome Day of the Lord. And it shall come to pass that whoever calls on the name of the Lord shall be saved. For in Mount Zion and in Jerusalem there shall be deliverance, as the Lord has said, Among the remnant whom the Lord calls.

Isaiah 13:9-13—Behold, the DAY OF THE LORD comes, cruel, with both wrath and fierce anger, to lay the land desolate; and He will destroy its sinners from it. For the stars of heaven and their constellations will not give their light; the sun will be darkened in its going forth, and the moon will not cause its light to shine. I will PUNISH THE WORLD for its evil, and the wicked for their iniquity; I will halt the arrogance of the proud, and will lay low the haughtiness of the terrible. I will make a mortal more rare than fine gold, a man more than the golden wedge of Ophir. Therefore I will shake the heavens, and the earth will move out of her place, In the wrath of the Lord of hosts and in the day of His fierce anger.

Acts 2:19-20—"I will show wonders in heaven above and signs in the earth beneath: Blood and fire and vapor of smoke. The sun shall be turned into darkness, and the moon into blood, BEFORE THE COMING of the great and awesome Day of the Lord. Compare with Matthew 24:29-31.

Mark 13:24-27—But in those days, AFTER THAT TRIBULATION, the sun will be darkened, and the moon will not give its light; the stars of heaven will fall, and the powers in the heavens will be shaken. Then they will see the Son of Man COMING IN THE CLOUDS (compare with Acts 1:9-11, Matthew 24:29-31, and Revelation 14:14) with great power and glory. And then He will send His angels, and gather together (rapture) His elect from the four winds, from the farthest part of earth to the farthest part of heaven.

Revelation 6:12-14—I looked when He opened the sixth seal, and behold, there was a great earthquake; and the sun became black as sackcloth of hair, and the moon became like blood. And the stars of heaven fell to the earth, as a fig tree drops its late figs when it is shaken by a mighty wind. Then the sky receded as a scroll when it is rolled up, and every mountain and island was moved out of its place.

Amos 8:8-12—Shall not the land tremble on this account, and everyone mourn who dwells in it, and all of it rise like the Nile, and be tossed about and sink again, like the Nile of Egypt? "And on that day," declares the Lord God, "I will make the sun go down at noon and darken the earth in broad daylight. I will turn your feasts into mourning and all your songs into lamentation; I will bring sackcloth on every waist and baldness on every head (compare with Isaiah 3:18-26); I will make it like the mourning for an only son and the end of it like a bitter day." "Behold, the days are coming," declares the Lord God, "when I will send a famine on the land—not a famine of bread, nor a thirst for water, but of hearing the words of the Lord. They shall wander from sea to sea, and from north to east; they shall run to and fro, to seek the word of the Lord, but they shall not find it."

Amos 5:18-20—Woe to you who desire the DAY OF THE LORD! Why would you have the Day of the Lord? It is darkness, and not light, as if a man fled from a lion, and a bear met him, or went into the house and leaned his hand against the wall, and a serpent bit him. Is not the Day of the Lord darkness, and not light, and gloom with no brightness in it?

Isaiah 13:6-7—Wail, for the Day of the Lord is at hand! It will come as destruction from the Almighty. Therefore all hands will be limp, every man's heart will melt.

1 Thessalonians 5:1-2—But concerning the times and the seasons, brethren, you have no need that

I should write to you. For you yourselves know perfectly that the DAY OF THE LORD SO COMES AS A THIEF IN THE NIGHT. Compare with Revelation 16:15.

2 Peter 3:10-12—But the DAY OF THE LORD will come as a thief in the night, in which the heavens will pass away with a great noise, and the elements will melt with fervent heat; both the earth and the works that are in it will be burned up. Therefore, since all these things will be dissolved, what manner of persons ought you to be in HOLY conduct and GODLINESS, looking for and hastening THE COMING OF THE DAY OF GOD, because of which the heavens will be dissolved, being on fire, and the elements will melt with fervent heat?

Malachi 4:5—Behold, I will send you Elijah the prophet BEFORE the coming of the great and DREADFUL DAY OF THE LORD. See also Matthew 17:11 and Zephaniah 1:14-18.

With regard to the evidence of these passages, can we now truly deny that these disastrous events of tribulation will occur after His people are taken (raptured) from the earth? Can one bring forth other biblical evidence that will disprove these beliefs?

Although the seven seals of Revelation 6 were provided as seen below, the main focus of these seals will be geared toward the events of the fifth and sixth seals, for if you notice, these particular seals, which the Bible speaks about, seem to take place before the coming of the Lord and the gathering (rapture) of His people. Many believe that the fifth seal of Revelation 6 refers to the 144,000 of the tribes of Israel or to those left behind after the taking (rapture) of His people. However, in the Bible, you will find no indication of any other white robe being worn except by the 24 elders (Revelation 4:4) and the great multitude of "all nations, tribes, peoples, and tongues" that had come out of the Great Tribulation, as stated in Revelation 7:9. Compare Revelation 6:9-11 with Revelation 7:9-14.

Revelation 6:9-11—When He opened the fifth seal, I saw under the altar the souls of those who had been slain for the word of God and for the testimony which they held. And they cried with a loud voice, saying, "How long, O Lord, holy and true, until You judge and avenge our blood on those who dwell on the earth?" Then a WHITE ROBE was given to each of them; and it was said to them that they should rest a little while longer, until both the number of their fellow servants and their brethren, who would be killed as they were, was completed.

Revelation 7:9—After these things I looked, and behold, a great multitude which no one could number, of all nations, tribes, peoples, and tongues, standing before the throne and before the Lamb, clothed with WHITE ROBES, with palm branches in their hands,

Revelation 7:13-14—Then one of the elders answered, saying to me, "Who are these arrayed in WHITE ROBEs, and where did they come from?" And I said to him, "Sir, you know." So he said to me, "These are the ones who come out of the great tribulation, and washed their robes and made them white in the blood of the Lamb."

Furthermore, if you take into account the increasing and unusual events of this present time—faltering economy, murders, suicides, deaths, and so on—they would seem to relate with several of the seals of Revelation 6.

First seal—Rider on white horse went about conquering and to conquer.

Second seal—Rider on the red horse takes peace from the earth that people should kill one another.

Third seal—Black horse: A quart of wheat for a day's wages and three quarts of barley for a day's wages (faltering economy, economic collapse, and famine).

Fourth seal—Pale horse: Death and Hades were given power to kill with sword, with hunger, with death, and by the beasts of the earth.

Fifth seal—Souls that were persecuted and slain for the word of God and its testimony.

Sixth seal—A great earthquake, the darkening of the sun, the moon turned blood red, and the stars of heaven fell to the earth. Compare this seal with Matthew 24:29-31 and Acts 2:19-20.

Seventh seal—There is silence in heaven for about half an hour (the completion of the opening of all seven seals).

In this paragraph, I briefly describe and illustrate the events of the sixth seal, which have led me to believe that the other seals of Revelation 6 will eventually occur before the coming of the Lord and the resurrection (rapture) of His people. Once the seal was opened, a massive earthquake took place, the sun became black as a sackcloth of hair, the moon became like blood, and the stars of heaven fell to the earth, as a fig tree drops its late figs when it is shaken by a mighty wind. As we compare these events with those that are written and spoken of by God's servants in Isaiah 13:10-13; Joel 2:31; Amos 5:18-20; Amos 8:9; Matthew 24:29; Mark 13:24; Luke 21:25; and Acts 2:19-20, it will seem to describe that the events of the sixth seal will take place "BEFORE THE COMING of the great and awesome Day of the Lord."

In Matthew 27, you will see several events that seem to symbolize and relate with the events of the fifth and sixth seals of Revelation 6. Matthew 27:45 describes a darkness that came upon the land during the time of Jesus's persecution (crucifixion). In Revelation 6:9, God's people will be persecuted and slain before the darkness comes upon the earth. But after Jesus gives up His Spirit in verse 50, an earthquake takes place, in the same manner the earthquake of Revelation 6:12 will come about, after the death of those who had held to the testimony of Christ. But notice that after His death, the darkness, and the earthquake, "the graves were opened; and many bodies of the saints who had fallen asleep were raised. Coming out of the graves after His resurrection, they went into the holy city and appeared to many" (Matthew 27:52 and 53). However, one notable part of this verse, which resembles that of the resurrection (rapture) is when "many Holy people" (not all) came out of the graves "After His Resurrection," in the same manner as will happen at the time of His Coming: persecution of God's people (Revelation 6:9–11), the great earthquake and darkness (Revelation 6:12), then the resurrection (rapture) of God's chosen people (Revelation 7:9-14 and Revelation 14:14-16), just as they took place in Matthew 27:52 and 53. Aren't we noticing a perfect picture of what is to take place during the time of the opening of these seals before the first resurrection (rapture)?

Therefore, if the events of the Sun, Moon, and Stars that are stated in the passages above are relevant to those written in Revelation 6:12-14 and spoken about by Christ in Matthew 24:29 and Mark 13:24, then be assured that times of tribulation will befall the people of the earth before the coming of the Lord and the taking up (rapture) of His people.

Further, 1 Corinthians 15:52 refers to the rapture of the church occurring at the sound of the last trumpet. There are no references in the New Testament that describe the sound of the last trumpet other than the seven trumpets of judgment found in Revelation 8, 9, and 11. Could this be evidence that the rapture of His people will not occur until a time of Tribulation has taken place? Compare 1 Corinthians 15:52 (the last trumpet) with the last trumpet of Revelation 11:15 and 11:18. See also Revelation 8:2; 8:6; 8:10; 8:12; 9:1; and 9:13.

1 Corinthians 15:52–In a moment, in the twinkling of an eye, at the last trumpet. For the trumpet will sound, and the dead will be raised incorruptible, and we shall be changed.

Revelation 11:15—Then the seventh angel sounded: And there were loud voices in heaven, saying, "The kingdoms of this world have become the kingdoms of our Lord and of His Christ, and He shall reign forever and ever!"

Revelation 11:18—The nations were angry, and Your wrath has come, And the time of the dead, that they should be judged, and that You should REWARD* Your servants the prophets and the saints, and those who fear Your name, small and great, And should destroy those who destroy the earth.

Therefore, if Revelation 11:15 is not referring to the last trumpet of 1 Corinthians 15:52, as many believe, then the New Testament should specifically refer to another last trumpet other than the last trumpet of Revelation 11:15. Could the rapture be the reward* that will be given to the prophets and saints after the sound of the last trumpet (v18)?

Mathew 16:27—For the Son of Man will come in the glory of His Father with His angels, and then He will reward* each according to his works.

Revelation 22:12—"And behold, I am coming quickly, and My reward* is with Me, to give to every one according to his work. *See also Matthew 16:27, Luke 6:23, Mark 9:41, and Revelation 22:12.

Chapter Ten

THE COMING THIEF

Now, to further support this conclusion, as you begin to read Revelation 16:1-14, you will become aware of the wrath that will come upon "those who had the mark of the beast and those who worshiped his image" (Rev. 16:2). But when you come to verse 15, notice how Christ's coming becomes evident during the time of God's wrath and the Great Tribulation. Compare Revelation 16:15 (His Coming), together with 1 Corinthians 15:23; 1 Thessalonians 4:15-17; 1 Thessalonians 5:23; 2 Peter 3:10-12; Matthew 24:29-31; Revelation 14:14-16; and Acts 2:19-20. (When reading the above final three passages, take particular note of the order of events occurring before His Coming).

Revelation 16:1-14—Then I heard a loud voice from the temple saying to the seven angels, "Go and pour out the bowls of the wrath of God on the earth." So the first went and poured out his bowl upon the earth, and a foul and loathsome sore came upon the men who had the mark of the beast and those who worshiped his image. Then the second angel poured out his bowl on the sea, and it became blood as of a dead man; and every living creature in the sea died. Then the third angel poured out his bowl on the rivers and springs of water, and they became blood. And I heard the angel of the waters saying: "You are righteous, O Lord, The One who is and who was and who is to be, Because You have judged these things. For they have shed the blood of saints and prophets, And You have given them blood to drink. For it is their just due." And I heard another from the altar saying, "Even so, Lord God Almighty, true and righteous are Your judgments." Then the fourth angel poured out his bowl on the sun, and power was given to him to scorch men with fire. And men were scorched with great heat, and they blasphemed the name of God who has power over these plagues; and they did not repent and give Him glory. Then the fifth angel poured out his bowl on the throne of the beast, and his kingdom became full of darkness; and they gnawed their tongues because of the pain. They blasphemed the God of heaven because of their pains and their sores, and did not repent of their deeds. Then the sixth angel poured out his bowl on the great river Euphrates, and its water was dried up, so that the way of the kings from the east might be prepared. And I saw three unclean spirits like frogs coming out of the mouth of the dragon, out of the mouth of the beast, and out of the mouth of the false prophet. For they are spirits of demons, performing signs, which go out to the kings of the earth and of the whole world, to gather them to the battle of that great day of God Almighty.

Revelation 16:15—"Behold, I am COMING as a thief. Blessed is he who watches, and keeps his garments, lest he walk naked and they see his shame."

2 Peter 3:10-12—But the day of the Lord will come as a THIEF in the night, in which the heavens will pass away with a great noise, and the elements will melt with fervent heat; both the earth and the works that are in it will be burned up. Therefore, since all these things will be dissolved, what manner of persons ought you to be in HOLY conduct and GODLINESS, looking for and hastening the coming of the day of God, because of which the heavens will be dissolved, being on fire, and the elements will melt with fervent heat?

Therefore, if Revelation 16:15 and 2 Peter 3:10-12 (I am Coming as a thief) refers to the Coming of the Lord and the rapture of His people, or the first resurrection, as evident throughout these passages, then be assured that times of Tribulation will unfortunately occur before His people are taken (raptured) from the earth.

In evaluating and referencing these and other passages from the Bible, it is evident that the church, despite its rejections and beliefs, will not be taken (raptured) until a time of Tribulation has taken place, as described in Matthew 24:29-31; Acts 2:19-20; Revelation 14:9-16; and Revelation 16:1-15.

As you may have well realized, my conclusion rests upon the belief that the church will be present during a time of the Great Tribulation. The reason for this belief comes not only from the sparse and weak evidence the church has presented up to the present time, but also from the visions, dreams, and revelations* I have received throughout the years concerning the order of these events. Therefore, I do urge that, if necessary, you reread and carefully look into the evidence of these chapters before denying or rejecting this belief, for your life, both physical and spiritual, will depend on it. Read See also Revelation 22:6; 2 Thessalonians 2:1–4; Revelation 3:10-11 along with the significant evidence from the many passages I have provided throughout this book.

*Consider the book, The Wrath, The Return, The Truth: Judgment Has Begun!

Chapter Eleven

THE ANTICHRIST:
A PROPHETIC SYNOPSIS

Now, as you turn to Ecclesiastes 1:9, it states, "What has been is what will be, and what has been done is what will be done, and there is nothing new under the sun." In addition, Ecclesiastes 1:10 states, "Is there a thing of which it is said, 'See, this is new'? It has been already in the ages before us."

Whether or not you understand the meaning of the above passages, they are merely stating what has taken place in the past and will take place in the future. It is another form of saying that history repeats itself. And you may ask, what could I gather from these verses and how do they relate to what is written here? Studying the events of certain chapters of the Old Testament, you will be able to get a glimpse of events that will lead up to the time of the end, eventually gaining insight into the meaning of the verses that are stated above.

In Genesis chapter 7, you will encounter a story about a man named Noah who sent out a raven that flew back and forth until the water receded from the earth. However, one intriguing part to this story, which I have found of interest, is that the Bible does not specify the purpose of the raven and what took place as it flew about, but rather emphasizes the actions of the dove. When I looked into the symbolism of the raven, I was surprised to find that it was defined as a devourer and a bird of prey within the crow family. This brought me to 1 Peter 5:8, which describes the adversary (Satan) as a roaring lion, seeking whom he may devour. Also, Malachi 3:11 states, "'And I will rebuke the devourer for your sakes, So that he will not destroy the fruit of your ground, Nor shall the vine fail to bear fruit for you in the field,' says the Lord of hosts."

The significance of the raven is that this bird, which was released at the end of 40 days, represents the figure that the Bible describes as the man of perdition and lawlessness. This man, who is also known to many as the Antichrist, will come upon the whole world to deceive and seek those whom he may devour. But as you read 2

Thessalonians 2 and relate it to several other biblical passages, you will acknowledge that he must be revealed before God's chosen people are taken (raptured) from the earth. Be advised that he, the deceiver, is active in the world in the present day, waiting for the time that God has appointed before he is able to be revealed.

Looking further into these passages, could the release of the raven (Genesis 8:7), better known as the devourer, have any connection to the appearance of the Antichrist during the worldwide event of Revelation 3:10?

With regard to the above, my understanding is that the possible time of the Antichrist's appearance and of his deceptions will come about 40 days after the occurrence of an economic collapse or a famine.

It should be noted that the raven, which is defined as a devourer (and is better known to many as Satan), was released 40 days after the flood. Similarly, as found in Matthew chapter 4, beginning with verse 1, Satan also appeared after Christ's 40-day fast, at the time of His hunger.

How do these passages relate to the time of the Antichrist's appearance and to his deceptions?

Satan, in the first temptation mentioned in Matthew 4:2-3, attempts to deceive Christ after His forty-day fast by tempting Him with bread. I am certain that, after a period of economic collapse, the Antichrist will take advantage of the opportunity to deceive people into accepting him in order to obtain food.

Matthew 4:2-3—And when He had fasted forty days and forty nights, afterward He was hungry. Now when the tempter came to Him, he said, "If You are the Son of God, command that these stones become bread."

If you compare the second temptation from Matthew 4:5 with 2 Thessalonians 2:4, you see that Satan, in the latter verse, not only appears at the temple, but deceptively also claims to be God.

Matthew 4:5—Then the devil took Him up into the holy city, set Him on the pinnacle of the TEMPLE.

2 Thessalonians 2:3-4—Let no one deceive you by any means; for that Day (His Coming and the gathering of His people) will not come unless the falling away comes first, and the man of sin is revealed, the son of perdition, who opposes and EXALTS HIMSELF above all that is called God or that is worshiped, so that he sits as God IN THE TEMPLE of God, showing himself that he is God. Compare 2 Thessalonians 2:1-3 (His Coming and the gathering) with Matthew 24:30-31 and Revelation 14:14-16.

Further, in comparing the third temptation of riches from Matthew 4:8-9 with Daniel 11:24, 30, and 32, you will become aware that certain riches will be given even to those who are unfaithful to God.

Matthew 4:8-9—Again, the devil took Him up on an exceedingly high mountain, and showed Him all the kingdoms of the world and their glory. And he said to Him, "All these things I will give You if You will fall down and worship me."

Daniel 11:24—He shall enter peaceably, even into the richest places of the province; and he shall do what his fathers have not done, nor his forefathers: he shall disperse among them the plunder, spoil, and RICHES; and he shall devise his plans against the strongholds, but only for a time. Also read the latter part of Daniel 11:30.

Daniel 11:32—Those who do wickedly against the covenant he shall corrupt with flattery; but the people who know their God shall be strong, and carry out great exploits.

Likewise, if we compare the three temptations stated in Matthew 4:1-9 (bread, temple, and riches) with the events that occurred around the time of the last supper of the Passover feast—see John 13:27, Luke 22:3-5, and Matthew 27:5 (bread, temple, and riches)—we see a certain similarity. Reading 2 Thessalonians 2:4 and Daniel 11:36, 37, and 43, we discover that the events stated in these passages are similar to those that the Antichrist will bring about.

Daniel 11:36-37—Then the king shall do according to his own will: he shall exalt and magnify himself above every god, shall speak blasphemies against the God of gods, and shall prosper till the wrath has been accomplished; for what has been determined shall be done. He shall regard neither the God of his fathers nor the desire of women, nor regard any god; for he shall exalt himself above them all. Relate with 2 Thessalonians 2:3-4.

Daniel 11:43—He shall have power over the treasures of gold and silver, and over all the precious things of Egypt; also the Libyans and Ethiopians shall follow at his heels. Relate with Matthew 4:8-9 and Daniel 11:24.

Furthermore, 2 Thessalonians 2:4 and 9-11 say that a "strong delusion" will occur at the time of the Antichrist's appearance, but are not specific about the details. Contemplating this chapter, I concluded that the deceptions mentioned here may not be the only "strong delusions" that will come. Reading these passages, you will see the Antichrist exalting himself in the temple, performing deceptive wonders and attempting to show himself to be God. As God's adversary, his prime objective will be to deceive not only the people of the world, but also those who acknowledge Christ. Many will fall for his deception and will, unfortunately, accept him as their savior, but those who know their God will do everything possible to oppose him. Looking further into these passages, I realized that there could be more to these deceptions than what is being made known to us. As I considered various possibilities, aside from the deception of the crucifixion scars on the Antichrist's hands, another strong delusion that could mislead even the elect came to mind. It concerns the biblical description of Christ's return.

In certain passages (Matthew 24:30, Matthew 26:64, Acts 1:9, Revelation 1:7, and Revelation 14:14), you will read that Christ, at the time of His coming, will appear in the clouds with power and great glory. While 2 Thessalonians 2:2-8 and Daniel 11:24, 30, and 32 tell us about the Antichrist's deception, would he not have to appear in the clouds in order to impersonate Christ's Coming and to bring about this "strong delusion"?

Additionally, the mark the Bible speaks about will likely not be an actual, visible mark that the people will receive on the hand or on the forehead. The placement of this mark, which <u>may be</u> figurative, will symbolize that one has accepted the Antichrist. This belief may seem somewhat speculative, but I ask, would you sacrifice your own salvation, knowing that you will voluntarily be receiving the mark of this beast (Antichrist)? Read Revelation 13:16-17, Exodus 13:9, and Deuteronomy 6:8 and 11:18.

Therefore, could the significance of these passages be that they are providing us with the time of the Antichrist's appearance and of his deceptions? Does the Bible contain and reveal such information? Read Revelation 13:18.

Chapter Twelve

CONCLUSION

At some point, a severe catastrophe will bring about the most terrifying events on earth that anyone has ever seen. Even today, one can look around and realize that both political and natural events have made the earth a dangerous place. The increase in natural disasters such as earthquakes, hurricanes, tsunamis, and floods, not to mention the rise in murders, suicides, international terrorism, plagues, and so on, is just the beginning of sorrows (read Matthew 24:7-8). You may wonder what other catastrophes or crises we should expect. While the Bible is not specific about a date, at a certain moment, when this time of financial tribulation has reached its climax and world leaders struggle to deal with the mounting calamities, a man of intrigue masquerading as the Son of God will appear. Millions will believe that his appearance is the fulfillment of prophecy. Unfortunately, it's not the Christ people expect, but the Antichrist masquerading as the Son of God. Many will fall into his deception, but the Bible states that those who know their God will do everything possible to oppose him (Daniel 11:32-37). The Bible states that we are obviously living the earth's final days. Will the people, particularly those in the church, be prepared for that final day?

America, nations, and people of the world, we are now on the verge of facing a calamity of great proportion, and what is ahead of us will, without prejudice, affect us all. Leaders and people of all nations, have you acknowledged the doomsday that lurks behind your door? Have you not taken into account the several nations that are presently suffering because of the scarcity of their food supply? The pain, sufferings, and hunger that the people, especially the children, of these nations have been facing due to disastrous events, government control, unemployment or economic hardship are just a few of the causes that have brought calamity, mass riots, and death upon them. Will New York City—the financial capital of the world—be exempt from any of these events? The current economic dilemma that is being felt in America and other nations is just a shadow of things to come. Will you be prepared? We've knelt in prayer seeking guidance, yet immediately rejected and denied the message that God has revealed to us. Will the precious lives of your children be sacrificed because of your rejections and unbelief? What can you lose if you prepare? If you don't prepare? What is gained if you prepare? But what is lost if you don't? A life! The time to do the right thing is now. Let us all get in a right relationship with God and one another now, before it is too late. Remember, this is not about religion, for religion is not the means to your salvation. This is about a personal relationship with Christ, the source to your salvation. Read Jeremiah 2:35 and Jeremiah 25:29-32.

This is our time to warn New York City and the rest of the world of the impending Day of Judgment, a day that seems to be drawing closer and closer. It is a time to call upon the people to repent of their sinful ways and turn to the ways of God. We must look back on the choices we have made, and evaluate the benefits and consequences. It's a time to look at the reflection with regard to all the events that took place in our lives, not only from our victories, but also from our failures. This is a time for understanding and a time for repentance. We know that God always watches over the earth and is always waiting for His people to repent. Have you been reflecting on the limitation of this time?

We cannot overlook the fact that all have been subjected to sin and have succumbed to it at one time or another. We live in a society plagued with the sins of abortion; homosexuality; adultery; fornication; child molestation; blasphemy; pornography; hatred; greed; lies; and so on. And the people of this age, including the churches and its leaders, live today just like in the days of the Judges in the Old Testament; they do what is right in their own eyes. The result is that people are calling evil things good and good things evil (Isaiah 5:20). There are so many signs of the end times today, in fact, that one would have to be either biblically illiterate or spiritually blind not to realize that we are living on borrowed time. And because of this, we must take the opportunity, but even more crucially, the responsibility, to reflect on our lives and come to repentance. For the consequences of not doing so will be inevitable. Read Galatians 4:16.

It has been and always will be the responsibility of God's people to present the gospel in its true and proper form to anyone and everyone we can. By evangelizing to the people, we can increase the possibility of our nation coming together to know the true Messiah. We as children of God are called to bring God's word in its truth, but the problem today is that very little in Christianity and other true religions are of the quality to provoke anyone to anything. Our witness is a powerful one and Satan would like nothing more than to destroy it. Thousands are being deceived and misled by unbiblical messages and false religions every day. Although certain religions believe they are the chosen and true doctrine over all doctrines, the true gospel is that which is preached by those who bring it in the name of our Lord Jesus Christ from its original and unedited text. But we should be ashamed of ourselves every time a cult member knocks on our door, or we see two clean-cut boys on bicycles working a neighborhood. They are more zealous for a lie than most of us are for the truth. We have no excuse. It is the sign of the times, the age we are living in right now, the age of the great commission, the age just prior to the coming judgment upon the earth and the calling away of God's chosen believers.

Revelation 22:6-7—Then he said to me, "These words are faithful and true. And the Lord God of the holy prophets sent His angel to show His servants the things which must shortly take place." "Behold, I am coming quickly! Blessed is he who keeps the words of the prophecy of this book."

Nations, could you expect to excel in economic prosperity when the laws you have permitted to be implemented are contrary to God?

Churches, it is suggested that you abstain from your self-beliefs, self-interpretations, judgments, and rejections. For the churches of the present day are prepared neither for His Judgment nor for His coming. Read Luke 10:16.

Matthew 22:14—"For many are called, but few are chosen. See also Matthew 15:8 and 9.

Church leaders, it is time to put things into perspective, for God will hold you accountable both for the lack of knowledge of His word and for the lives of those He has placed in your hands.

Revelation 22:19—and if anyone takes away from the words of the book of this prophecy, God shall take away his part from the Book of Life, from the holy city, and from the things which are written in this book.

1 Thessalonians 5:20-22—Do not despise prophecies. Test all things; hold fast what is good. Abstain from every form of evil.

Now may the God of hope fill you with all joy and peace in believing, that you may abound in hope by the power of the Holy Spirit.

Information of Interest

Having an ample supply of provisions is an essential part to one's preparedness. A selected number of manufacturers of long shelf life provisions (20+ years) are: MountainHouse.com, BePrepared.com* (1-800-999-1863), GrandmasCountry.com (1-800-216-6466), and

Resourcefull.ShelfReliance.com (1-877-743-5373). The Mountain House brand is also available at BePrepared.com. *Request free monthly catalog.

If the provisions are supermarket bought, be certain that all items and expiration dates are printed on paper and not saved to PC. Also, remember to stock up on other regularly used items.

To ensure preparedness, consider the purchase of a handheld water purifier. A commendable unit to consider is the "*First Need" water purifier. *Replacement filters are also available. For added protection, purchase several "Steri-pen" pre-filters. This recommended filter can be placed on certain "Nalgene" wide-mouth water bottles. For additional information, or to purchase any of these products, Visit BaseGear.com.

DO NOT UNDERESTIMATE THE UNLEASHING POWER OF OUR PRESENT-DAY WORLDWIDE OCCURRENCES!

CPSIA information can be obtained at www.ICGtesting.com
Printed in the USA
269786BV00001B/2/P